KOREA

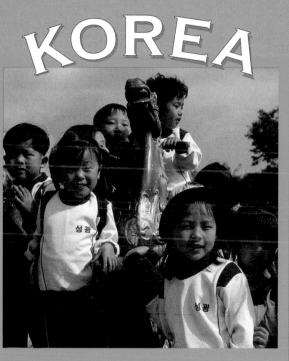

A TRUE BOOK

by
Elaine Landau

Children's Press®
A Division of Grolier Publishing

New York London Hong Kong Sydney
Danbury, Connecticut

Reading Consultant
Linda Cornwell
Coordinator of School Quality
and Professional Improvement
Indiana State Teachers
Association

Author's Dedication
For Derrick Kessler

A South Korean girl

Visit Children's Press® on the Internet at:
http://publishing.grolier.com

Library of Congress Cataloging-in-Publication Data

Landau, Elaine.
Korea / by Elaine Landau.
      p.   cm. — (A True book)
   Includes bibliographical references and index.
   Summary: A basic overview of the history, geography, climate, and culture of North and South Korea.
   ISBN: 0-516-20984-1 (lib. bdg.)   0-516-26766-3 (pbk.)
1. Korea—History—Juvenile literature. 2. Korea (South)—Juvenile literature. 3. Korea (North)—Juvenile literature. [1. Korea. 2. Korea (South) 3. Korea (North)] I. Title. II. Series.
DS907.4.L36   1999
951.9—dc21   98-37359
                                                                          CIP
                                                                          AC

GROLIER
PUBLISHING

Contents

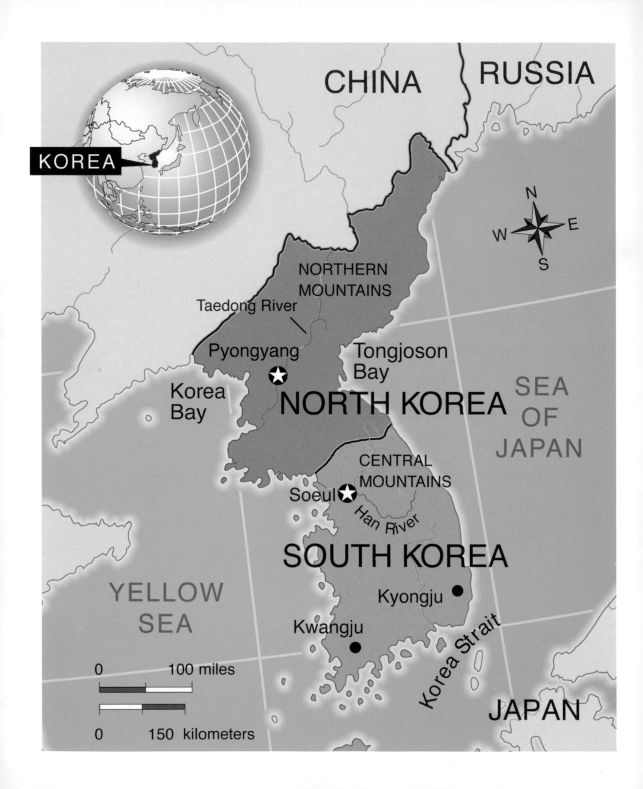

Land of the Morning Calm

Korea is a mountainous country in east Asia. It is located on the Korean Peninsula. This strip of land points south from northeast China. More than three thousand small islands off of Korea's south and west coasts are also considered part of the country.

Korea was once a single country. But now it is divided into two nations. They are North Korea (Democratic People's Republic of Korea) and South Korea (Republic of Korea).

North Korea has an area of 46,540 square miles (74,900 square kilometers). It is a bit larger than South Korea. South Korea has an area of 38,330 square miles (61,686 km). But more people live in South

An aerial view of Seoul, the capital of South Korea

Korea. Its capital city, Seoul, has a population of more than ten million. Six other South Korean cities have more than one million people.

Korea's climate varies greatly depending on the sea-

son. Summers are warm.
Winters are long and cold. The
rainy season in Korea lasts
from June to August. During
this time, parts of Korea
receive more than 30 inches
(76 centimeters) of rain.

Some people think the most
interesting feature of Korea is
its mountains. Much of central
North Korea is blanketed by
mountains. Many have trees or
shrubs growing at their peaks.
They are often seen in paintings of the Korean countryside.

Mt. Kumgang-San (left) is located in North Korea. Mist-covered mountains (below) may have helped Korea become known as the "Land of the Morning Calm."

Korea was once known as Choson, which means "Land of the Morning Calm." Looking at the tree-covered mountains in the morning mist, it is easy to see why.

Korea's History

People have lived in Korea for thousands of years. At various times, Koreans have had to overthrow foreign invaders. In 1910, Japan seized control of Korea. But when Japan was defeated in World War II (1939–45), it lost Korea. In 1948, Korea was divided into

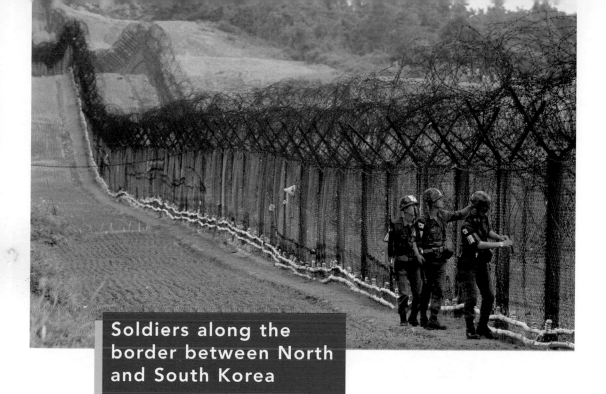

Soldiers along the border between North and South Korea

two separate nations: North Korea and South Korea. North Korea became Communist. South Korea did not.

The countries have not remained peacefully separated. In 1950, North Korea attacked

In this 1950 photograph, soldiers from the United Nations move through the streets of Seoul, South Korea.

South Korea hoping to take it over. The Korean War began. The United States and other nations aided South Korea in its struggle against Communism. China and the Soviet Union, both Communist countries, assisted North Korea.

The war ended in 1953. But there was no clear victory for either side. A peace treaty was never signed. Meanwhile, the uneasiness between the two countries continued. Sometimes fighting broke out again.

After a while, the situation improved. Government leaders from North and South Korea

North Korean leaders (left) shake hands with South Korean leaders (right) during a 1989 meeting to try to improve life for families in both countries.

began a series of talks to try to work things out. In 1991, they signed an agreement to end the use of force between them.

Facts About North Korea

A view of Pyongyang, North Korea's capital

Official Name: Democratic People's Republic of Korea

Capital: Pyongyang

Official Language: Korean

Area: 46,540 square miles (74,900 square kilometers)

Population: 24 million

The North Korean flag

The Governments

The governments of North Korea and South Korea are quite different from each other. In South Korea, a president elected by the country's people heads the government. Members of South Korea's National Assembly—the country's lawmaking body—are also elected by the people.

In this 1998 photograph, lawmakers begin to gather for meetings in South Korea's National Assembly.

The president selects a prime minister to see to the daily running of the government. There are also state council members who are appointed by the president. These individuals lead different government departments.

At times in its history, the South Korean government has severely limited its peoples' rights. During the 1970s and 1980s, people who opposed the government were often jailed. In May 1980, South Korean protesters were attacked by the military. Large numbers of people were killed. The incident became known as the Kwangju Massacre. In October 1980, a new constitution, or set of laws for a nation, was approved. It allows South

This 1996 photograph shows about five thousand people gathered to remember the protesters who were killed in the 1980 Kwangju Massacre.

Koreans to more openly express themselves.

North Korea also has a president. Its main lawmaking body is called the Supreme People's Assembly. But the government is really controlled

The Supreme People's Assembly meets in this building in Pyongyang, North Korea.

by the nation's Communist Party.

There is still no real freedom of speech or of the press (television, newspapers, radios, and magazines) in North Korea. To keep a firm grip on the country's people, the Communist Party also limits many of their other rights and freedoms.

How the People Live

At one time, most Koreans were farmers who lived in small villages. Families that included grandparents, parents, children, aunts, and uncles often lived all together.

However, both North and South Korea have experienced many changes. Now many

This small farming village (above) is located in Kyong-ju, South Korea. Seoul (left) is one of South Korea's busiest cities. Here, people crowd the city's Nandaemun Market.

South Koreans live in large cities. Their homes are usually in high-rise apartment buildings or brick or concrete houses. They often move to the city because of the many jobs provided by businesses there.

South Korean cities also frequently have fine hospitals, universities, and libraries. For entertainment, there are many restaurants and nightclubs.

Many North Koreans also live in cities. North Korea's most important city is Pyongyang, its capital. City dwellers are often factory workers who live in

A North Korean family in their small apartment in Pyongyang

small apartments. Usually only important Communist officials have houses in the cities. Unlike South Koreans, most North Koreans do not own cars. North Korean cities also lack the different kinds of restaurants and entertainment found in South Korean cities.

Large numbers of farmers in North Korea live on farms called collectives. There, many farmers work the land and raise livestock together.

These women on a collective farm in North Korea are tending young corn and rice crops.

This woman (left) and man (right) are dressed in traditional Korean clothing.

Most North and South Koreans dress like people in the United States. But at times traditional Korean clothing is worn. Traditional dress for Korean women includes a long, full skirt called a *chima*. It is worn with a *chogori*—a short, tight jacket tied with a bow. Traditionally dressed men wear loose-fitting pants with a loose jacket that can be tied with a bow.

Many traditional Korean foods are quite popular. Kimchi is made with spicy, hot pickled vegetables. Spicy soups are enjoyed as well. Many Koreans do not eat as much meat as fish. Nearly everyone eats rice. Rice is served with a variety of foods.

Koreans also frequently eat beans, sweet potatoes, and

A waitress prepares a meal for businessmen (above) in a South Korean restaurant. A couple (right) enjoys ginseng tea at a teahouse in Seoul, South Korea.

fruits such as peaches, pears, and melons. Tea has been drunk in Korea for thousands of years. But many Koreans also enjoy coffee.

As in the United States, sports are enjoyed in both North and

South Korea. Baseball, basketball, table tennis (Ping-Pong), wrestling, skating, and archery are played in South Korea. Many people there also practice tae kwon do—a two-thousand-year-old method of self-defense.

Baseball (left) is a favorite sport in both North and South Korea. This tae kwon do class (below) in South Korea is taking place outdoors.

In North Korea, physical fitness and sports are encouraged at government-owned gyms. The government has also sponsored teams for weight lifting, boxing, wrestling, mountain climbing, and other sports. At various times, athletes from both North and South Korea have won medals at the Olympics. (The Summer Olympics were held in Seoul, South Korea, in 1988.)

While sports are enthusiastically played in North and South

The students in this South Korean classroom are participating in an art lesson.

Korea, education is believed to be especially important. South Korea has both public and private schools. Depending on students' abilities and interests, they may prepare to go to college or to learn a trade.

In North Korea, students who wish to attend school past the tenth grade must be approved by the Communist Party. There is one university in North Korea and many colleges that teach a specific subject area such as engineering or law.

Religious practices vary in Korea. Most South Koreans follow the teachings of Confucius and Buddha. These teachings stress how people should behave toward one another.

Some South Koreans are Christians.

Religion is strongly discouraged in North Korea by the Communist Party. The Communists believe that religion might interfere with Communist teachings.

The Economy

Industry has grown in South Korea in the last fifty years. Its fast-growing economy has made it an important country in world trade. Among the many products manufactured in South Korea are textiles, clothing, processed foods, chemicals, machinery, ships, cars, computers, and paper.

Workers in a South Korean clothing factory (left),
Fishing boats gathered in a harbor near the border
of North and South Korea (right)

Fishing is also important to
South Korea's economy.
Oysters, pollack, and other
fish are common in South
Korea's waters. A large num-
ber of farmers are fishermen

as well. But when farming, many grow rice—the country's largest crop. Melons, Chinese cabbage, soybeans, sweet potatoes, and other foods are also grown.

In North Korea, some of the products that are manufac- tured include: cement, textiles, processed foods, chemicals, and machinery. Among the nation's most important crops are rice, wheat, corn, and barley. As in South Korea, fishing is also an important source of income.

However, in the late 1990s, there were severe food shortages caused by drought and flooding conditions. The United Nations World Food Program sent food and supplies to various North Korean sites.

Facts About South Korea

Official Name: Republic of Korea

The grounds of a former palace in South Korea

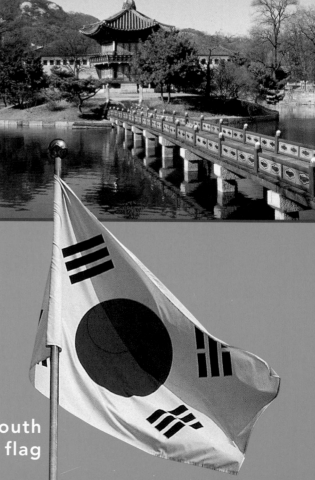

Capital: Seoul

Official Language: Korean

Area: 38,330 square miles (61,686 square kilometers)

Population: 46 million

The South Korean flag

Art and Culture

Koreans are proud of their country's long tradition of art and culture. Beautiful wall paintings have been discovered on the tombs of ancient Korean rulers. Magnificently crafted crowns and statues also lie within these burial sites.

These folk dancers (above) are performing at an outdoor festival in South Korea. This South Korean artist (left) is hand painting a newly made vase.

Korean painters, writers, and sculptors have been praised throughout the world. Korean music and dance has delighted audiences for centuries.

Traditional dances are performed with slow movements. But Korean folk dances are quite lively. The hour-glass drum, bells, gongs, flutes, and stone chimes are among Korea's traditional instruments.

A North Korean musician plays the flute.

This theater group is performing in the Children's Palace in Pyongyang, North Korea.

In North Korea, most types of entertainment are government controlled. Artists are not as free to express themselves as artists in South Korea. However, government-approved plays and operas can be seen in large North Korean cities. And traveling theater groups tour the countryside.

Both North and South Korea have a long history. There is much for people in both countries to be proud of. However, both countries continue to face problems. Hopefully, the future will include prosperity and peaceful relations between them.

To Find Out More

Here are some additional resources to help you learn more about the nations of North Korea and South Korea:

 **Books**

Climo, Shirley. **The Korean Cinderella.** HarperCollins, 1993.

Demi. **Buddha.** Henry Holt & Co., 1996.

Gay, Kathlyn and Martin Gay. **Korean War.** Twenty-First Century Books, 1996.

Han, Suzanne Crowder. **The Rabbit's Escape.** Henry Holt & Co., 1995.

Heo, Yumi. **The Green Frogs: A Korean Folktale.** Houghton Mifflin, 1996.

Loewen, Nancy. **Food In Korea.** Rourke Publications, 1991.

Solberg, S. E. **The Land and People of Korea.** HarperCollins, 1991.

Organizations and Online Sites

Korean Cultural Service
2370 Massachusetts
  Avenue NW
Washington, DC 20008

Korean Embassy
http://korea.emb.washington.dc.us/new/frame/

Here you'll find current events, speeches, and information about travel in Korea. Sign the guestbook!

Korea at a Glance
http://www.knto.or.kr/1korea/index1.htm

This site contains a map and a lot of information about Korea.

The Korea Herald
http://www.koreaherald.co.kr/

Headline news, weather, sports, classified ads, editorials, and everything else you would expect to find in a daily newspaper.

North Korea Maps
http://darkwing.uoregon.edu/~felsing/kstuff/nkmaps.html

Access all kinds of maps, including satellite images, weather maps, street maps of major cities, and more.

United Nations
Department of Public
  Information
New York, NY 10017

Young Hoon Elementary School
http://younghoon-e.ed.seoul.kr/e-index.html

Find out what it's like to be a student at a school in South Korea. Learn about academics, activities, and holidays. Send mail!

Important Words

Buddha an Indian teacher who founded Buddhism and taught unselfishness and kindness to others

climate the usual weather in a place

Communism a social system in which a country's industry is owned by the government and there are no social classes

Confucius a Chinese philosopher who founded Confucianism and taught that all people should respect each other

economy the way a country runs its industry, trade, and finance

oppose to resist or be against

peace treaty formal agreement between nations to end fighting or conflict

prosperity success

Index

Meet the Author

Elaine Landau has a Bachelor of Arts degree in English and Journalism from New York University and a Masters degree in Library and Information Science from Pratt Institute. She has worked as a newspaper reporter, children's book editor, and a youth services librarian, but especially enjoys writing for young people.

Ms. Landau has written more than one hundred nonfiction books on various topics. She lives in Miami, Florida, with her husband Norman and son, Michael.